Putting
The
One
Minute
Manager
to Work

Also available from Fontana:
The One Minute Manager Kenneth Blanchard, PhD
and Spencer Johnson, MD (1983)

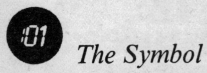 *The Symbol*

The One Minute Manager's symbol –
a one minute readout from the face of
a modern digital watch – is intended to
remind each of us to take a minute out
of our day to look into the faces of the
people we manage. And to realise that
they are our most important resources.

Putting The One Minute Manager to Work

How to turn the 3 Secrets into Skills

Kenneth Blanchard, Ph.D.
Robert Lorber, Ph.D.

Fontana/Collins

First published in Great Britain by Willow Books 1984
First issued in Fontana Paperbacks 1984
Fourth impression April 1985

Made and printed in Great Britain by
William Collins Sons & Co. Ltd, Glasgow

Contents

TO

Our wives, Margie and Sandy,
for their constant love
and support throughout
the highs and lows
of our lives

Introduction

In the last episode of *The One Minute Manager*, the bright young man who was searching for an effective manager learned the One Minute Manager's three secrets. He immediately realised that they were the key to effective management.

The young man learned the One Minute secrets well, because eventually the inevitable happened: he became a One Minute Manager.

He set One Minute Goals.

He gave One Minute Praisings.

He delivered One Minute Reprimands.

In this second episode of *The One Minute Manager*, a veteran manager wonders whether using the three secrets on a day-to-day basis will really make a difference where it counts – in performance. Bothered by this question, he seeks the answer from a new One Minute Manager. In the process he learns how to put the One Minute Manager to work in a systematic way to achieve excellence.

This book is meant to be a companion to the original book. It is a practical tool that can be used independently to implement the three secrets of the One Minute Manager but will probably be a richer experience if you have first read *The One Minute Manager*.

We hope you apply and use what the veteran manager learns and see if it doesn't make a difference in your life and the lives of those who work with you.

Kenneth Blanchard, Ph.D.
Robert Lorber, Ph.D.

Putting The One Minute Manager To Work

W HEN the veteran manager finished reading *The One Minute Manager*, he put the book down on his coffee table. He leaned back with a questioning look. He had first read the book at the office but had brought it home to give it another reading.

'Even after a second time through', he thought to himself, 'I cannot argue with the logic of the three secrets of the One Minute Manager. But if I practise them, will I actually become a more productive manager?'

The veteran manager decided to do something about his question. The next morning he would telephone a manager in a town some distance away who had, in recent years, turned a troublesome company into a very profitable enterprise. The veteran had read a newspaper interview with this manager in which he had credited much of his success to practising One Minute Management. In fact, he now called himself a 'One Minute Manager'.

T HE next morning when the veteran manager got to his office, he rang the new One Minute Manager. He introduced himself and asked the manager if he could see him at some time that week and talk about One Minute Management. The veteran had been warned what the answer might be but he was still surprised when the One Minute Manager actually said, 'Come any time except Wednesday morning. That's when I meet with my key staff. To be honest with you, I don't have much scheduled this week. I'll be glad to talk to you.'

'I'll be there tomorrow morning at ten', said the veteran manager, chuckling to himself. When he put down the phone he thought, 'This ought to be interesting. I'm sure I'll get my questions answered.'

When the veteran manager arrived at the One Minute Manager's office, the secretary said, 'He's expecting you. Go straight in.'

As he entered the room, he found a man in his late forties standing by the window looking out.

The veteran manager coughed and the One Minute Manager looked up. He smiled and said, 'Good to see you. Let's sit down over here.' He led the manager to a pair of comfortable chairs in the corner of the room.

'Well, what can I do for you?' the One Minute Manager asked as he sat down.

'I have read *The One Minute Manager* and so have my staff', the veteran manager began. 'I'm enthusiastic about it and so are they, but that has happened before when a new management system has been introduced. My question is how do you put One Minute Management to work in a way that turns the secrets into usable skills and makes a difference where it really counts – in performance?'

'Before I attempt to answer that question', said the One Minute Manager, 'let me ask you one. What do you think the message of One Minute Management is?'

'It's quite simple', said the veteran manager. 'If you have a sheet of paper I'll write it down for you.'

The One Minute Manager went over to his desk and got a pad. He gave it to the veteran manager. Without pausing the veteran manager wrote:

*

*People Who Produce
Good Results*

*Feel Good
About Themselves*

*

'That's an interesting twist', said the One Minute Manager, gesturing to a plaque on the wall behind his desk. It read: *"People Who Feel Good About Themselves Produce Good Results"*. 'Why did you change it?' he asked.

'I think it represents more accurately the essence of One Minute Management', insisted the veteran manager, 'and besides, it's more consistent with what you teach'.

'Consistent?' questioned the One Minute Manager.

'Yes', responded the veteran manager firmly. 'You say that one of the key ingredients to a One Minute Praising is to be specific – to tell the person exactly what he or she did right.'

'That's true', said the One Minute Manager.

'Then praisings, which help make people feel good about themselves, are not effective unless those people have done something positive first', smiled the veteran manager, feeling he had the One Minute Manager trapped.

'You're a tough man', laughed the One Minute Manager, 'and you really have a good idea about what One Minute Management is all about. I think I can learn a few things from you. I'll feel good about sharing as much as I can with you.'

'I doubt if you will learn much from me', said the veteran manager. 'I'm just a "street fighter" who has survived.'

'Can't take a compliment, is that it?' mused the One Minute Manager. 'Most people can't quite accept being praised.'

'I would imagine that's because we've never had much practice receiving praisings', said the veteran manager. 'And it's not easy to do something that you're not used to doing, even if you believe in it.'

'Right', said the One Minute Manager. 'One of the reasons it's hard to implement One Minute Management is that people will have to change some of their old behaviour. And focusing on and changing how people treat each other in organisations is something that only gets lip service. Most top managers think that management training is just a fringe benefit – a nice little frill they can give all their employees every year. That's why I have that saying on the wall', he said as he gestured to a plaque on the other side of the room. It said:

*

*Most Companies
Spend All Their Time
Looking For Another
Management Concept
And
Very Little Time
Following Up The One
They Have Just Taught
Their Managers*

*

'That's so true', said the veteran manager. 'And people do the same thing. They're always looking for the next "quick fix" rather than using what they have already learned. They go from one diet programme to another diet programme, one exercise plan to another without following the last plan.'

'Then they wonder why they don't lose weight or build up their heart', said the One Minute Manager. 'It reminds me of a story of the man who slipped and fell off a cliff while hiking on a mountaintop. Luckily he was able to grab a branch on his way down. Holding on for dear life, he looked down to see a rock valley some fifteen hundred feet below. When he looked up it was twenty feet to the cliff where he had fallen.

'Panicked, he yelled, "Help! Help! Is anybody up there? Help!"

'A booming voice spoke up. "I am here and I will save you if you believe in me".

'"I believe! I believe!" yelled back the man.

'"If you believe in me", said the voice, "let go of the branch and then I will save you".

'The young man, hearing what the voice said, looked down again. Seeing the rock valley below, he quickly looked back up and shouted, "Is there anybody else up there?"'

'That's a good one', laughed the veteran manager. 'That's exactly what I don't want to do – hold onto the branch and keep looking for another system. One Minute Management is the way I want to manage and be managed. All I want to know is how to put it to work so that it lasts and makes a difference.'

'Then you came to the right place', said the One Minute Manager. 'What problems have you been having using the three secrets?'

'I think the main difficulty I have experienced', said the veteran manager, 'has been turning the secrets into skills. That is, knowing when to do what. For example, sometimes I think I'm reprimanding when I should be goal setting and at other times I'm goal setting when I should be reprimanding.'

'I had the same trouble', said the One Minute Manager, 'until I learned my ABC's'.

'I know you're not talking about the ABC's of school days', said the veteran. 'So what do you mean?'

'NO, I'm not referring to the alphabet, but the ABC's are a way of getting back to basics. They've helped this organisation make the transition from secrets to skills. We knew the three secrets of One Minute Management, and we were really enthusiastic, but they weren't working for us in day-to-day performance until we learned the ABC's of management', said the One Minute Manager. Picking up his notepad he wrote:

> A = Activators
> B = Behaviour
> C = Consequences

Then he began his explanation:

'*A* stands for *activators*. Activators are those things that have to be done by a manager before someone can be expected to accomplish a goal. *B* stands for *behaviour* or performance. It is what a person says or does. *C* stands for *consequences* or what a manager does after someone accomplishes or attempts to accomplish a goal. If managers can learn to understand and deliver the necessary activators (A) and consequences (C), they can ensure more productive behaviour (B) or performance.'

'So learning your ABC's is a key to performance', said the veteran.

'It certainly is', said the One Minute Manager. 'A number of companies throughout the country have realised that they can experience significant performance improvement by following up and getting their managers to actually use the ABC's and other implementation strategies I'll teach you. And what's interesting about these companies is that they are from a variety of businesses and industries – banking and finance, construction, communication, energy utilisation, high technology, hotels and restaurants, and retail merchandising. And they worked on all kinds of performance areas including productivity (both quality and quantity), safety, staff retention, sales, costs and profits. In every case real "bottom line" improvements were experienced.'

'You've got my interest', said the veteran manager. 'I think I'd better learn more about the ABC's if I want to put One Minute Management to work and make those kinds of differences.'

'Why don't you go and see one of my staff, Tom Connelly', said the One Minute Manager. 'He took over a work group that averaged nearly a 50 per cent annual staff turnover. Now it's down to less than ten per cent. He can tell you all about the ABC's.'

'I'd love to meet him', said the veteran manager. 'But before you ring him, let me ask you one more thing. Do you always talk in threes? First three secrets and now ABC's.'

'Not always', smiled the One Minute Manager. 'But I believe in the KISS method: "Keep it short and simple". I don't think people can remember a whole lot of things, particularly if they are going to use what they have learned.'

'Isn't KISS usually "Keep it Simple Stupid"?' wondered the veteran manager.

'Yes', admitted the One Minute Manager. 'But since One Minute Management is a positive approach to managing people, we use a positive way to express the concept.'

'I knew you'd have a good explanation', smiled the veteran. 'I'm looking forward to meeting Connelly.'

The One Minute Manager dialled a number and said, 'Tom, I have an experienced manager here who wants to learn his ABC's. Are you free?'

Although the veteran could not hear everything clearly, he smiled as he thought he heard Connelly say, 'Send him over. I've just got back. I was out having fun catching my people doing things right.'

'Come back and see me when you've finished talking to Tom', said the One Minute Manager as he led the veteran manager to the door.

'Certainly', said the veteran manager. 'Thanks for your time.'

WHEN the veteran manager got to Connelly's office, he found a smartly dressed man in his mid-forties.

As Connelly got up from his desk and introduced himself, the veteran manager got right to the point: 'Your boss told me you could give me the real low down on the ABC's of management'.

'I'll try', said Connelly. 'Let me start off by giving you this summary that we use so everyone can remember their ABC's.' He handed the veteran manager a chart.

THE ABC's OF MANAGEMENT:
A Summary

The term:

A	B	C
ACTIVATOR	**BEHAVIOUR**	**CONSEQUENCE**

What it means:

What a manager does *before* performance	Performance: What someone says or does	What a manager does *after* performance

Examples:

One Minute Goal Setting ●Areas of accountability ●Performance standards ●Instructions	●Writes report ●Sells shirt ●Comes to work ●Misses deadline ●Types letter ●Makes mistake ●Fills order	*One Minute Praising* ●Immediate, specific ●Shares feelings *One Minute Reprimand* ●Immediate, specific ●Shares feelings ●Supports individual *No response*

The veteran manager read the chart very carefully. When he finished reading he looked up, smiled and said, 'So One Minute Goal Setting is an activator?'

'Yes', said Connelly. 'An activator is like an "ante" in poker. It gets things started.'

'If goal setting is an activator', said the veteran, 'then you're not in the management game unless your staff are clear on their key areas of responsibility (accountability) and what good performance in each of those areas looks like (performance standards)'.

'That's why goal setting is the most important activator for managers to remember', said Connelly. 'It starts the whole management process.'

'Sounds good', affirmed the veteran manager. 'Once people are activated, then they are ready to perform.'

'They certainly are', said Connelly. 'It's that performance that managers need to watch. Once you have asked someone to do something, what they say or do while trying to accomplish the desired task is their performance or behaviour – the *B* of ABC's.'

'Is what people think or feel considered to be behaviour?' asked the veteran manager.

'No', said Connelly. 'While thoughts and feelings are important since they often determine what people do, they are not considered behaviour because they are behind the eyeballs.'

'In other words', jumped in the veteran, 'you cannot see them'.

'Right', said Connelly. 'Once you get into thoughts and feelings, there's lots of room for complications and misunderstanding. If we stick to behaviour, things are clearer because behaviour can be observed and measured. As you can see from the chart, writing a report, selling a shirt, coming to work on time, missing a deadline, typing a letter, making a mistake and filling an order are all behaviours.'

'From that list, it seems that behaviour can be either desirable or undesirable', commented the veteran manager.

'Right', said Connelly. 'And how easily you are able to distinguish between the two depends on the goal setting process. You see, if One Minute Goal Setting is done properly, the desired performance is stated in behavioural terms – that is, it can be seen (observed) and counted (measured). That is important because when you observe someone's behaviour you want to be able to determine whether it is contributing towards the accomplishment of the goal (they are doing things right), or taking away from goal achievement (they are doing things wrong). That gives you an idea of how to respond as that person's boss.'

'Respond?' said the veteran manager.

'Responding has to do with consequences', said Connelly. 'The *C* in our ABC's. They are the responses managers give to people when they either perform a task or attempt to perform a task. Consequences follow or come after some performance.'

'One Minute Praisings and One Minute Reprimands are obviously consequences', said the veteran manager.

'A One Minute Praising is an example of a positive consequence or response', said Connelly, 'while a One Minute Reprimand is an example of a negative response. Whether positive or negative, the consequence has to be appropriate.'

'Appropriate?' wondered the veteran manager.

'If you want people to stop doing something, give them a negative response like a One Minute Reprimand', said Connelly. 'But if you want people to keep doing something, or to improve or learn something new, give them a positive consequence like a One Minute Praising.'

'I find that using praisings and reprimands appropriately is not always easy', said the veteran manager.

'It certainly isn't', said Connelly. 'One of the problems is that many managers seem to praise or reprimand their staff depending on how they themselves feel on any given day, regardless of anyone's performance. If they are feeling good, they pat everyone on the back, and if they are in a bad mood, they yell at everyone.'

'And I would imagine that if managers start doing that – praising and reprimanding indiscriminately – their credibility will soon be questioned', said the veteran manager.

'Good point', commented Connelly. 'It reminds me of the story about the blind man who is walking down the street with his guide dog. They get to a corner and while they are waiting for the lights to change, the dog lifts his leg and pees on the blind man's trouser leg. When that happens, the blind man reaches into his pocket and takes out a dog treat. Then he bends down and looks as if he is about to give it to the dog. A bystander who has seen this whole thing can't contain himself any longer so he goes up to the blind man and says, "Sir, it's probably none of my business but I noticed that your dog took a leak on you and now you are about to give him a treat. Do you think that is really a good idea?" The blind man smiles and says, "I'm not about to give my dog a treat. I just want to find out where his head is so I can kick him in the tail." '

'That's beautiful', laughed the veteran. 'When people see a manager isn't credible, that is confusing to them. If the blind man gave the dog a treat for inappropriate behaviour like that and yelled at him when he really wasn't doing anything wrong, the dog would soon become confused and not know what to do. I have seen confusion like that in organisations. Therefore I'd better make sure I understand about consequences.'

'Good idea', said Connelly.

'As I told the One Minute Manager', continued the veteran manager, 'my problem is more confusion about when to be reprimanding and when to be goal setting than any difficulty between reprimanding and praising. Do you have any suggestions?'

'Yes', said Connelly. 'Remember you can effectively reprimand only those who are winners because you can end your negative feedback with a praising like: "You're one of my best people – this recent performance is so unlike you". You can't do that with people who are learning to perform and therefore have no past good performance history.'

'So what do you do when people who are learning make a mistake?' queried the veteran.

'I would go back to goal setting and start again. You can summarise it this way', said Connelly, writing on his pad of paper:

When To Reset Goals
And
When To Reprimand

If a person:

CAN'T DO *something → Go Back to Goal Setting*
(*A Training Problem*)

If a person:

WON'T DO *something → Reprimand*
(*An Attitude Problem*)

'That's very helpful', said the veteran. 'So you never reprimand learners.'

'No', said Connelly, 'or you will immobilise them and make them even more insecure'.

'So reprimands do not teach skills', observed the veteran manager. 'They can just change attitudes – get skilled people back to using their abilities.'

'Precisely', said Connelly. 'After you reset goals with someone you are training, you don't leave that person alone. Observe the performance again and then either praise progress or go back to goal setting once more.'

'It seems to me from what you're saying', commented the veteran, 'that there are five steps to training a learner to be a good performer:

1) Tell *what* to do
2) Show *how* to do
3) Let person try
4) Observe performance
5) Praise progress or Redirect

'You've got it in one', said Connelly. 'That's a good summary of how to train someone.'

'What if you keep redirecting some of your staff again and again and they just don't show any progress?' questioned the veteran manager.

'You talk to such a person about career planning', laughed Connelly. 'In other words, he or she just might not be in the right job.'

'Given the importance of redirecting in training', said the veteran, 'why don't you list it as a consequence on your ABC chart?'

'That's a good question', said Connelly. 'Redirect certainly does follow behaviour. But I never thought of it as a consequence. I'll have to add it.'

'I see from the chart, though', said the veteran, 'that you have no response listed as a consequence'.

'It's the most popular with managers', said Connelly. 'So often managers simply ignore their staff's performance, and it doesn't work.'

'What do you mean?' said the veteran manager.

'What happens if you get no response from performing a task?' asked Connelly. 'If your manager doesn't do or say anything?'

'In the beginning, I'd try harder', said the veteran. 'I'd think, "If only I try harder maybe my boss will notice".'

'What if your boss still didn't notice or respond?' asked Connelly.

'After a while, I'd start doing it "half-fast" ', smiled the veteran, getting into the pun game that the One Minute Manager and his staff seemed to enjoy. 'Since no one seems to care whether I do this or not, why kill myself.'

'Unless you were doing something that was motivating to you in and of itself', said Connelly.

'If that occurred you would be confused about the difference between work and play', said the veteran manager.

'That's an interesting way to put it', said Connelly. 'If you are doing what you enjoy at work, you will continue to do it well regardless of whether anyone notices and pats you on the back. But generally, no response to good performance, like a negative consequence, tends to decrease the possibility of that performance being repeated.'

'Let me see if I have this straight', said the veteran manager as he showed Connelly his notes:

*

*Only
Positive
Consequences
Encourage
Good
Future
Performance*

*

'That's about it', said Connelly, 'and yet, how do managers most frequently respond to their staff's performance?'

'Negative or no response at all', said the veteran manager. 'As we both know, the attitude of most managers seems to be: when people perform well, do nothing. When people make a mistake, complain.'

'It's the old "leave alone–rebuke" technique', said Connelly. 'Not a very effective way of motivating people.'

'But a very easy habit to fall into', said the veteran manager. 'I've done it myself. I can see now that if I'm going to manage my staff, I'd better learn to manage consequences.'

'That's an important lesson to learn', said Connelly. 'Most people think that activators have a greater influence on performance than consequences. And yet, only 15 to 25 per cent of what affects performance comes from activators like goal setting, while 75 to 85 per cent comes from consequences like praisings and reprimands.'

'You're saying that what happens after a person does something has more impact than what happens before?' questioned the veteran sceptically.

'That's it', said Connelly. 'Performance is determined mainly by consequences. That's why the One Minute Manager is so vehement about the importance of follow-up. We believe you should spend ten times as much time following up your management training as it took to plan and conduct an initial programme. Otherwise people will revert back to old behaviour in a short period of time.'

'Yes, but if you don't set goals, it's unlikely that people will do what you want them to do in the first place', interjected the veteran manager.

'Right', said Connelly. 'But goal setting without any managing of consequences – praising good performance and reprimanding poor – will only get things started and short term success for a manager. In other words, managers will get the performance they want only when they are there, but when they are not there, people may or may not engage in the desired behaviour. We have a saying that emphasises the importance of managing consequences', said Connelly, pointing to a wall plaque.

*

*As A Manager
The Important Thing
Is Not What
Happens When You Are There
But
What Happens When
You Are Not There*

*

'That's so true', said the veteran. 'I can always get the performance I want from people, even from my kids at home, when I am there. But I'm not around all the time. In fact, I think I spend as much, if not more, time at work with my fellow managers at the same level in the organisation and with my boss as I do with my subordinates.'

'So the way you can really tell how good a manager you are', said Connelly, 'is not by what happens when you are there, but by what happens when you're not there. And the secret to getting good performance from your staff when you're not there is how effectively you deliver consequences when you are there – both praisings and reprimands.'

'It is clear to me now', said the veteran manager, 'what you meant when you said activators are important for starting good performance – getting it done the first time – but what really determines and influences whether that desired performance will be repeated when you are not there is what happens after the original performance. The "leave alone–rebuke" approach just frustrates and alienates people.'

'The whole purpose of teaching our people their ABC's', said Connelly, 'is to ensure that they sequence One Minute Goal Setting, One Minute Praisings, and One Minute Reprimands in the proper order. It's a behavioural reminder.'

'You certainly showed me how to begin to turn the secrets into skills', said the veteran. 'I don't think I'll ever forget when to do what any more. But let me ask one more question. You have been emphasising the importance of clear, good goal setting, followed by One Minute Praisings for good performance. I seem to have lost the idea of the effective use of One Minute Reprimands. All we have been talking about is the misuse of reprimands. Could you share with me some of the positive use of reprimands again?'

'You might want to talk to the One Minute Manager about the effective use of One Minute Reprimands', said Connelly. 'He loves to teach that secret, and besides, he would be willing to answer any questions you have about One Minute Goal Setting and One Minute Praisings as well.'

'That's a good idea', said the veteran manager. 'I certainly have taken up enough of your time.'

'That's OK', said Connelly. 'I have enjoyed it. Besides, knowing my ABC's has really helped to give me more free time.'

'I hope it does the same for me', said the veteran.

As the veteran manager left Connelly's office, he found his mind going a mile a minute. Connelly had been quite helpful. As he approached the One Minute Manager's office, the manager's secretary smiled. 'Did you have a good meeting with Tom Connelly?' she asked.

'I certainly did', the veteran manager replied, returning her smile. 'Could I see the boss?'

'Go straight in', she said. 'He was wondering if you were coming back.'

As the veteran entered the office, he found the One Minute Manager looking out of his favourite window. He turned as he heard the veteran manager enter.

'You were with Connelly for quite a while. The two of you must have got along quite well', he said.

'It was most helpful', said the veteran. 'But I have some concerns about the use of reprimands', he went on. 'In teaching me the ABC's, Connelly seemed to stress the importance of praisings but played down the use of reprimands. I know you believe in delivering bad news sometimes. Maybe I just need some reorientation.'

'The best way for me to respond to your concerns about reprimanding', replied the One Minute Manager, 'is to start by talking about managing winners – people with proven track records. Winners are easy to supervise. All you have to do is set up One Minute goals and then they are off.'

'It's the same in my experience', said the veteran manager. 'While everyone likes a pat on the back once in a while, you don't have to praise winners very much. They usually beat you to the punch. Apart from not praising winners very much, you don't often have to reprimand them either, do you?'

'No!' said the One Minute Manager. 'Good performers are usually self-correcting. If they make a mistake, they fix it before anyone else notices.'

'But everyone makes mistakes sometimes that they are unaware of', stated the veteran manager.

'In that case, you may have to reprimand', said the One Minute Manager. 'However, good performers don't resent it because of the way you deliver that reprimand if they know the three secrets.'

'I assume you are talking about ending the reprimand with a praising', wondered the veteran manager.

'Precisely', said the One Minute Manager.

'Connelly cleared up for me why you don't reprimand a learner, but I still have trouble understanding why you praise someone at the end of a reprimand', said the veteran manager.

'Remember, you reprimand only when you know the person can do better', the One Minute Manager reminded him. 'When you leave your staff after a reprimand, you want them to be thinking about what they did wrong, not about the way you treated them.'

'I don't understand', the veteran hesitated.

'Let me see if I can explain it this way', said the One Minute Manager. 'Most people not only don't end their reprimands with a praising, but they also give the person a parting shot: "If you think you're going to get promoted, you have another think coming". Now when you leave that person, especially if there is a co-worker within earshot, what do you think they will be talking about? How you treated the person you were reprimanding, or what the person did wrong?'

'How you treated the person', said the veteran manager.

'Precisely', said the One Minute Manager. 'They're talking about how awful you are. And yet that person did something wrong. If you end your reprimand with a praising, you will be telling the person, "You are OK but your behaviour isn't!" Then when you leave, the person will be thinking about what he or she did wrong. If for any reason he tries to complain about you to co-workers, they will stop it by saying, "What are you getting so excited about? He said you were one of his best people. He just doesn't want you to make that mistake again."'

'I think I understand what you're saying about ending with a praising', said the veteran manager. 'See if this is a good summary comment', as he showed his notes to the One Minute Manager. They said:

*

When You
End A Reprimand
With A Praising
People Think
About Their *Behaviour*
Not
Your Behaviour

*

As the One Minute Manager read what the veteran had written, he smiled and said, 'That's very well put. Let me give you a personal example to illustrate the importance of what you are saying. One Friday night, shortly after I had learned about the One Minute Reprimand, my wife came into the room where I was reading the evening paper. I always know that there is something wrong and I am about to get the problem dumped in my lap when she says, "Great manager of people . . ." That's exactly what she said that night. Then she continued, "I just caught Karen (our 15-year-old daughter) sneaking out of the house with a bottle of vodka on the way to a party. She said it wasn't for her; it was for her older friends."

'"The drivers!" I guessed.

'"I think I'll kill her", said my wife. "Could you take over?"

'My wife and I always had a strategy: if one of us felt out of control of a situation, we threw the ball to the other. I have a lot of sympathy for single parents who have no one to turn to in such situations.

'Since I had just learned about the reprimand, I thought this might be a good opportunity to see if it worked. I said, "Where is Karen?" My wife told me she was in the kitchen. So I went straight out to the kitchen and found Karen standing there looking as though she were about to be sent to prison. I walked up to her and put my hand gently on her shoulder. I said, "Karen, Mum tells me she just caught you sneaking out of the house with a bottle of vodka. Let me tell you how I feel about that. I can't believe it. How many times have I told you the way kids get killed is to have some kid drinking and driving. And to be sneaking around with a bottle of vodka . . ."

'Now I knew that the rule of the reprimand was that you have only about thirty seconds to share your feelings.'

'I bet you wanted two hours', said the veteran manager.

'How right you are', laughed the One Minute Manager. 'Some parents take a whole weekend. You catch one of your kids doing something wrong on Friday night and you give the kid a row. Half an hour later you see the same kid and you say, "Let me tell you one other thing . . ." Then you see the kid the next morning and you say, "Let me tell you about your friends too . . ." You spend the whole weekend making yourself and the kid miserable over one misbehaviour.

'The rule about the reprimand is that you have only thirty seconds to share your feelings about what the person did wrong, and when it's over – it's over. Don't keep nagging the person for the same mistake.

'Recognising all this, I had to come to a screeching halt in sharing my feelings with Karen. It was at this point that I realised the importance of pausing for a moment of silence between sharing your feelings and the last part of the reprimand. It permits you to calm down and at the same time lets the person you are reprimanding feel the intensity of your feelings. So I took a deep breath while Karen was swallowing hard. Then I said, "Let me tell you one other thing, Karen. I love you. You're a really responsible kid. Mum and I normally don't have to worry about you. It sounds like some other kid. You're better than that. That's why Mum and I are not going to let you get away with that kind of thing."

'Then I gave her a hug and said, "Now get off to the party, but remember: you're better than that".'

'I'm not sure I would have let her go to the party after something like that', said the veteran. 'I bet she couldn't believe it herself.'

'She couldn't believe it', confirmed the One Minute Manager. 'But I told her, "Now you know how I feel about teenage drinking and sneaking around. I know you're not going to do that again, so have a good time."'

'In the past, before I knew about the One Minute Reprimand, not only would I not have ended her reprimand with a praising, I would have sent her to her room, screaming something like "You're not going to another party until you're twenty-five".'

'Now, if I had sent her to her room, what do you think she would have been thinking about? What she did wrong or how I had treated her?' said the One Minute Manager.

'How you had treated her', said the veteran manager. 'I bet she would have been on the phone immediately, telling her friends what a monster you were. Teenagers love to share parent stories.'

'Absolutely', said the One Minute Manager. 'And then she would have been psychologically off the hook for what she had done wrong, with all her attention focused on how I had treated her.'

'What happened next?' asked the veteran, feeling he was in the middle of a soap opera.

'The next morning', continued the One Minute Manager, 'when I was eating breakfast, Karen came downstairs. Wondering how I had done, I said to her, "Karen, how did you like the way I dealt with the vodka incident last night?"

' "I hated it", she said. "You ruined the party for me."

' "I ruined the party for you?"

' "Yes", she said. "Because all through the evening I kept thinking about what I had done and how much I had disappointed you and Mum!"

'I smiled to myself and thought, "It worked! It really worked! She was concentrating on what she had done wrong and not on how I had treated her." '

'That was a very helpful, clear example', said the veteran manager. 'I think I've got that part of the reprimand, but I'd like to ask you a couple of other things about the One Minute Reprimand.'

'Fire away', said the One Minute Manager. 'Most of the questions we get about One Minute Management have to do with the reprimand.'

'What if the person you are reprimanding – Karen, for example – starts to argue with you?' said the veteran.

'You stop what you are saying right away', said the One Minute Manager, 'and make it very clear to that person that this is not a discussion. "I am sharing my feelings about what you did wrong, and if you want to discuss it later, I will. But right now this is not a two-way discussion. I am telling you how I feel."'

'That's helpful', said the veteran. 'One other thing. If I accept the principle of praising someone at the end of a reprimand, why not begin a reprimand with a praising? When I did reprimands in the past, I used the "sandwich approach": pat them on the back, kick them, pat them on the back.'

'I know that style well', said the One Minute Manager, 'but I've learned that it is very important to keep praisings and reprimands separate. If you start a reprimand with a praising, then you will ruin the impact of your praising.'

'Why?' asked the veteran manager.

'Because when you go to see a person just to praise him', said the One Minute Manager, 'he will not hear your praising because he will be wondering when the other shoe will drop – what bad news will follow the good'.

'So by keeping praisings and reprimands in order, you will let your staff hear both more clearly', summarised the veteran. 'What about more tangible punishments like demotion, being transferred, or some other penalty? Are they ever appropriate?'

'Our experience with the One Minute Reprimand', said the One Minute Manager, 'suggests that you do not usually need to add some additional penalty. It is an uncomfortable enough experience.'

'That was beautifully illustrated with Karen', said the veteran manager. 'I think you really cleared up my questions about reprimands. And also now, I can see how learning the ABC's helps managers take their knowledge of One Minute Management and translate it into action. But how can you integrate One Minute Management into a total organisational programme for performance improvement?'

'You have to pay the PRICE', said the One Minute Manager with a smile.

'What is that?' asked the veteran manager.

'The PRICE system', said the One Minute Manager, 'goes beyond the ABC's by providing managers with five easy-to-follow steps that can involve everyone in improving performance'.

'It sounds fascinating', said the veteran, 'but my head is already swimming from all that I have learned today'.

'Why don't you stay overnight locally and we can get together at nine in the morning? I'll ask my secretary to make a reservation for you at the Osborn Hotel. The manager there is really excited about One Minute Management and has implemented a unique praising programme designed to catch his employees doing things right. I think you will find it most interesting.'

'Sounds good to me', said the veteran.

WHEN the veteran manager arrived at the hotel, he went straight to the registration desk. As he was checking in, the receptionist said to the veteran, 'Our customers are important to us. I wonder if I can ask you to do us a favour during your visit?'

'Of course', said the veteran, surprised by this request. 'What is it?'

'We'd like you to take this book of "praising coupons". If any of our employees treats you or another guest the way you like to be treated, would you tear off a coupon, write on the back what the employee did right, find out what his or her name is, and hand it in at the manager's office.'

'So all your customers are catching your employees doing things right', laughed the veteran. 'I bet a praising comes with each coupon the manager receives.'

'You read *The One Minute Manager*', exclaimed the receptionist with a smile.

'I did. Your hotel really seems to be putting One Minute Management to work', said the veteran.

'It's a fantastic system!' responded the receptionist enthusiastically. 'Have a nice evening.'

After an early dinner, the veteran went straight to his room to relax. He was amazed by how well he had been treated by all the hotel employees. He had already filled in three coupons - for the porter, his waitress, and the maitre d'hotel. Catching people doing things right was changing his whole attitude towards this hotel. The praising coupons made it his job as a guest not to complain but to compliment.

The next morning, the veteran manager packed his bags and headed downstairs. After having breakfast he checked out. On his way out of the hotel, he called in at the manager's office to drop off his praising coupons. The manager happened to be there.

As he handed the manager his praising coupons, the veteran manager said, 'I think this praising programme of yours is a great idea. It's a very practical way to put One Minute Management to work. Have there been any tangible bottom line effects of the programme?'

'Although we have had the system in operation for only five months or so', said the hotel manager, 'we have already seen significant reductions in absenteeism and staff turn-over. Our employees look forward to coming to work now because they are anxious to see if they can be caught doing something right. And we have not been giving any financial payoffs for coupons - just a pat on the back for a job well done.'

'Do you think this programme has changed the customers' attitudes, too?' wondered the veteran.

'Absolutely!' said the hotel manager. 'Our greatest improvement has been in guest inspection scores. Our guests are asked to rate the hotel on an ABCDE scale on such items as value/cost, appearance, service, and friendliness. Prior to the praising programme, less than 70 per cent of the guests who filled out the guest inspection cards rated the hotel in the A to B range. After the first five months of the programme the scores are averaging over 90 per cent A's and B's and we are getting three times as many returned cards.'

'So your praising coupons are paying high dividends for you, your customers, and your employees', said the veteran manager.

'Yes', said the hotel manager. 'Putting the One Minute Manager to work pays a good return on investment.'

As the veteran manager shook hands with the hotel manager, he smiled and said, 'My stay here has been very profitable for me too!'

WHEN the veteran arrived at the One Minute Manager's office, he found him in his usual pose by the window. When he sensed the veteran standing in the doorway, the One Minute Manager turned round and greeted him with a friendly handshake and offered the veteran a chair at the conference table.

'Well, did you enjoy your stay at the Osborn Hotel last night?' the One Minute Manager asked as he sat down.

'I certainly did', responded the veteran, 'and you were right – it was unique!'

'I wanted you to experience', confided the One Minute Manager, 'an attempt to put One Minute Management to work before we talked today. I thought it would help you understand our PRICE system better.'

As the veteran manager was listening to the One Minute Manager, he noticed a new plaque on his desk. It read:

*

Don't Just Do Something –
Sit There

*

The veteran manager smiled because he knew how the usual frantic, yet inefficient, pace of most organisations demanded the opposite.

'My key people gave it to me', said the One Minute Manager, when he saw the veteran looking at the plaque. 'They thought it symbolised the importance of goal setting as a means of avoiding the "activity trap".'

'The activity trap?' wondered the veteran manager.

'That's where people are running around trying to do things right before anyone has stopped to work out what are the right things to do.'

'Talking about doing things right', said the veteran, 'what's the best way for me to learn PRICE?'

'Why don't you go and talk to Alice Smith', suggested the One Minute Manager. 'She's one of our most creative managers. She helped us develop the PRICE system. Since she took over our sales operation, sales have skyrocketed.'

As the One Minute Manager was ringing Alice Smith, the veteran manager was smiling to himself. He thought, 'They certainly have taken all the mystique out of managing people. I'll bet PRICE is really quite simple, but powerful.'

'Well, Alice is all set to see you', said the One Minute Manager. 'You can go over to her office straight away. She is in the same building as Connelly but on the third floor.'

WHEN the veteran manager got to Alice Smith's office, he found her working quietly at her desk. He thought to himself, 'At last a One Minute Manager who seems to be doing some work'.

She smiled as he entered. 'So you want to know if the PRICE is right', she said as she beckoned the veteran to sit down.

'Corny but true', said the veteran. 'I'm anxious to get started.'

'That's important because the PRICE system is the nuts and bolts of how to put the One Minute Manager to work and make a difference every day with the performance and satisfaction of people on the job. But you have to listen carefully because now we take the basic three skills and turn them into five important steps.'

Smith immediately went to the small blackboard behind her desk and wrote:

Pinpoint
Record
Involve
Coach
Evaluate

'*Pinpoint* is a process of defining key performance areas for people in observable measurable terms', started Smith. 'In essence, it is the performance areas that you would identify as One Minute Goals.'

'Suppose I told you I had a morale problem in my work group', said the veteran manager, 'and I wanted to rekindle commitment from my staff. Would that be specific enough?'

'No', said Smith. 'We can't do anything about morale problems, poor attitudes, laziness, or things like that.'

'Isn't it important to deal with morale problems in organisations?' asked the veteran manager.

'Of course it is, but I would have to pinpoint what you mean by poor morale', explained Smith. 'Do you mean people are coming to work late, or quality rejects are frequent, or people are bickering at work? What do you mean by poor morale?'

'So we need to stop managers from saying things are good or bad', said the veteran, 'and get them to identify specifically what is happening'.

'That's what pinpointing is all about', said Smith, pleased by the veteran's ability to learn quickly. 'Establishing the areas you are going to measure and how you are going to measure them – for example, quantity, quality, cost (on or off budget), or timeliness.'

'Where does that bring us?' interrupted the veteran.

'Direct to *Record*', answered Smith. 'Once you have pinpointed a performance problem or One Minute Goal, you want to be able to measure present performance and keep track of progress in that area.'

'You mean you would gather actual data on how often people are late to work, how frequently products are rejected because of quality, and the like?' said the veteran.

'That's right', said Smith. 'You want to take the guesswork out of performance improvement.'

'What if someone says "You can't measure performance in my job!"' wondered the veteran manager.

'When people tell us that', said Smith, 'we suggest that maybe we should eliminate their position and see if we've lost anything. It's amazing how interested they suddenly get in establishing ways to identify goals and measure performance in their job.'

'Could you give me an example', said the veteran, 'of a performance problem you eliminated through the PRICE system?'

'Yes', said Smith. 'When I took over the department, the old sales manager told me, "The problem here is phone contact. Salespeople never make appointments with customers by phone. They think they have to be on the road all the time. When they get to the customer, he's often out for the morning, or he's busy and can't be interrupted. They have to wait to see him so they end up spending all their time in coffee shops. If they made appointments, they'd get twice as much done in half the time."

'I asked, "How do you know phone contact is a problem?"

'"I just feel all the problems start there", he replied. "That's always been a problem in this company."

'Then I asked, "Have you counted it? Is there any way to tell exactly the number of phone calls salespeople make to customers?"

'"Well", he said, "I could check their phone logs. Each salesperson is required to keep a daily log of calls beside his or her phone."

'When I checked it, I found that making appointments was not a crucial issue for everyone. In fact, only three salespeople were delinquent in their phoning', Smith stated.

'By recording or measuring performance', said the veteran, 'you attempt to make sure the problem is real and not just a feeling. You don't want to fix what isn't broken.'

'Precisely', said Smith. 'It's most effective to plot the information on a graph', she explained as she pulled a folder from her desk file. 'Here's an initial graph I made of appointment calls for one of my problem salespeople, Jack.

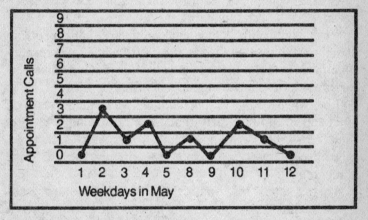

'On any of the graphs we use, we put time across the bottom or horizontal axis, and the pinpointed behaviour along the side or the vertical axis', explained Smith. 'The time element for Jack was weekdays in May for a two-week period and the behaviour was the number of appointment calls made each day.'

'After I made the graph I calculated Jack's mean number of daily appointment calls. Over two weeks, he averaged one call a day. I knew we had a problem and that there was a difference between actual performance and what I thought was desired performance. I was ready for the *Involve* step in PRICE.'

'Is that when you inform Jack about the problem?' questioned the veteran manager.

'Yes', said Smith. 'Once you are aware that a problem exists, you share that information with whoever is responsible (accountable) for that area and/or can influence performance in it – in our example it would be Jack.'

'I bet when you've graphed all this performance data on Jack and it shows clearly that he is not doing what you think he should be doing, there's a real temptation to let Jack have it', observed the veteran. 'Give him the old "leave alone–rebuke".'

'There often is', said Smith, 'but you need to control yourself. The time for reprimanding hasn't come yet. In fact, it is important to remember that graphs are not meant to be used as weapons, or as evidence in a managerial prosecution. They are designed to be used as training tools as well as non-judgmental methods of feedback.'

'So how do you share your graph with Jack?' asked the veteran.

'Without judgment', said Smith, 'and in a spirit of learning. You want Jack to learn, and you assume that Jack wants to improve. You know the saying here:

*

*Feedback
Is The
Breakfast
Of
Champions*

*

'How true that is', affirmed the veteran. 'But tell me, how do you involve someone like Jack besides giving him feedback on results?'

'You involve him in establishing the activators', said Smith. 'That is, deciding what has to be agreed upon before Jack can be expected to improve his performance to the desired level.'

'Besides goal setting, what other agreements do you have to set up?' smiled the veteran, enjoying the opportunity to show off what he had already learned.

'Coaching and evaluation strategies', answered Smith. 'You need to agree about how you are going to supervise Jack as well as how he will be evaluated and what pay-off he can anticipate for improved performance.'

'Do you always involve your people in establishing One Minute Goals?' wondered the veteran manager.

'Yes', said Smith. *One Minute Management just doesn't work unless you share it with your staff.* Otherwise they will think you are trying to manipulate them. That is particularly true with goal setting. Shared goal setting tends to get greater commitment from people and guarantees the setting of a realistic goal for the performance area.'

'A realistic goal?' puzzled the veteran manager.

'A realistic goal is moderately difficult but achievable', explained Smith. 'It's acceptable to you as a manager and it's possible for your members of staff to accomplish. Let's go back to Jack. He has been setting up one appointment a day by phone. How many appointment calls are acceptable to you? How many are attainable by Jack?'

'How many does the best salesperson make?' inquired the veteran manager.

'Comparing Jack to the best won't encourage him. It will only discourage him', answered Smith. 'Remember we're using this method as a training tool, not as a punishment.'

'What goal would you set?' asked the veteran, shrugging his shoulders.

'I'd probably say, "Jack, let's see if you can make three appointment calls a day next week. How does that sound?"'

'So you have to be specific about the number and the time span', commented the veteran.

'Exactly', said Smith. 'What do you suppose would happen if I simply said to Jack, "I'd like you to make more appointment calls. I don't think you have been making enough lately."?'

'He'd probably say OK', said the veteran, 'and then not take it seriously'.

'That's why I'd make a graph with Jack by my side', said Smith. 'Then he'd know I was serious and know exactly what he had to do to get back into my good books.'

She removed another graph from the file she had taken from her desk. 'This was Jack's first goal setting graph', said Smith as she handed the veteran the graph.

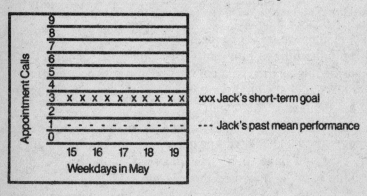

xxx Jack's short-term goal

--- Jack's past mean performance

'You see, we plotted Jack's past mean performance (one call a day) and his short-term goal (three calls a day). That way he could see the difference between what he'd been doing and where he was going', explained Smith.

'Why wouldn't you say you wanted Jack to make an appointment call for every sales visit he was going to make?' wondered the veteran.

'That might have been an appropriate goal in the long-term', said Smith, 'but in the short-term you couldn't expect that kind of turnaround in behaviour because Jack had obviously got himself into some bad work patterns. In the same way, you can't expect to lose twenty-five pounds in weight in one day, but you do want some change. So we had to set a short-term goal with Jack, like three appointment calls a day.'

'Short-term goal?' wondered the veteran.

'It's a first step', said Smith. 'When you set up a per-formance-improvement programme with someone, re-member not to set the end-result goal (in this case an appointment call for *every* sales visit – about six or seven calls per workday) as the goal that has to be reached before someone can feel a sense of accomplishment and deserve a praising; otherwise you might have to wait forever.'

'I remember that concept now', said the veteran. 'In the beginning, when working on performance, you need to set things up so you can catch people doing things approxi-mately right (short-term goal), not exactly right (final goal).'

'Precisely', said Smith. 'The journey to exactly right is made up of a whole series of approximately rights.'

'So you are saying, "Rome wasn't built in a day"', said the veteran. 'As a result, what you want to do is keep track of progress from the present level of performance to the desired level. What's the best way to do that?'

'By involving people in coaching', said Smith. 'As you know, once people have a clear idea about what they are being asked to do, coaching is essentially observing their performance and giving them feedback on results. But the whole coaching process is set up by agreeing in advance with your staff when and how you are going to give them feedback. That part of coaching is done during the *Involve* step.'

'I would imagine', interrupted the veteran, 'that by designing, together with your staff, the feedback system you are going to use, you are increasing the chances of their winning – accomplishing their goals'.

'Exactly', said Smith. 'Setting up a good feedback system through performance graphs is crucial if you hope to do any day-to-day coaching. That's why, with Jack, we agreed that for the first week I'd go and see him at his desk every day and review his phone log. I'd graph his performance and share it with him.'

'What other agreements about coaching did you make with him besides your daily visits?' wondered the veteran manager.

'Recording performance every day can be time-consuming', said Smith. 'So we agreed to meet again after the first week to evaluate when Jack could begin to administer his own feedback.'

'Administer his own feedback?' repeated the veteran.

'If I am having a performance problem with Jack, what I want to do is set up a graph that Jack is able to use. He can put his own check marks, stars, or whatever, on the graph.'

'Then he's able to say, "Hey, I'm doing better", or "I'm doing worse" ', suggested the veteran manager. 'He can even begin to praise or reprimand himself.'

'Yes', said Smith. 'Feedback that is self-administered can be immediate – as close to the performance as possible.'

'At this point, what else did you involve Jack in?' said the veteran.

'All I had left to do in the *I* step in the PRICE system was to involve Jack in performance evaluation', said Smith.

'How did you intend to do that?' asked the veteran manager.

'When we set up the graph, Jack knew how his perform-ance was going to be evaluated, but to complete his involve-ment in performance evaluation, we still had to decide what was in it for Jack if he improved', said Smith.

'What do you mean?' asked the veteran.

'What positive consequence will happen for Jack if he reaches his goal', Smith answered.

'Did I hear you say that you and Jack had to decide together? Don't you just tell him?' responded the veteran.

'If Jack had been less capable and committed, I would have determined the rewards, but Jack was a very creative man. He knew best what rewards would motivate him', explained Smith. 'I asked Jack, "What will motivate you to make more calls?" He said, "If I make my quota, write me a note. I collect those things. I have every letter of commendation I've received since school. But don't get your secretary to type me some form letter. You write it by hand."

'I thought that was a great idea. I said, "What if you don't meet your quota?" He said, "Come and tell me I deserve a reprimand. You probably won't even have to deliver it. But just knowing that you know I am slipping back to old behaviour will get me back on track."'

'Did you keep track of the number of praisings versus the number of reprimands?' laughed the veteran.

'It might sound funny', said Smith, 'but I did exactly that. I started a log of praisings and reprimands. It worked beautifully. Now I keep a praising/reprimand log on all my employees. It's just a list of names with P's and R's after each name with a shorthand note about what happened. It helps me keep track of One Minute Management.'

'That makes sense', said the veteran manager. 'So prior to actually coaching or evaluating performance, the consequences for goal accomplishment have to be agreed upon in the Involve (I) step of the PRICE system.'

'In Jack's case', said Smith, 'he knew what the goals (short- and long-term) were, how I was going to supervise or coach him, and how his performance would be evaluated, including the consequences he could expect for poor performance as well as for improved performance'.

'Now that all those things were settled', interrupted the veteran, 'Jack was ready to start improving his appointment-call behaviour'.

'Yes', said Smith. 'And at that point, my role changed from involving Jack in decision-making about establishing the necessary activators to observing his performance and managing the consequences.'

'That's what coaching is all about', said the veteran. 'Observing behaviour and giving feedback on results – both praisings and reprimands. And that's when you began the *C* or *Coach* step in PRICE.'

'You've got it. Now I can show you how well Jack did', said Smith. 'Here's his graph from the first week.'

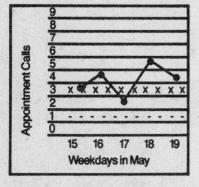

xxx Jack's short-term goal

--- Jack's past mean performance

'That's great. He bettered his goal except on the third day', commented the veteran manager as he read the graph. 'When did you tell him about his improvement – at your planned meeting at the end of the week?'

'Absolutely not', said Smith. 'Remember a basic rule of feedback is that it should be immediate and specific. If the data flow is vague and delayed, it is not an effective training tool. And besides, I had made an agreement with Jack that during the first week I'd go and see him every day, review his phone log, graph his performance and share it with him.'

'How specific would you be?' wondered the veteran manager.

'I'd actually use numbers', said Smith. 'I'd say, "You made your goal, you bettered your goal by one or you missed your goal by one". So once the goal is set, feedback relates specifically to the goal.'

'OK. I see how the daily feedback with Jack went', said the veteran, 'but how did you handle the meeting at the end of the week when you planned to evaluate whether Jack could begin to administer his own feedback or not?'

'I was happy with Jack's progress that first week', said Smith, 'so I was willing to listen to any suggestions he might have about how I should monitor his performance and give him feedback. Remember, as people improve, you want to gradually hand over more and more of the responsibility for monitoring their own performance to them.

'Jack was very much aware of his needs', went on Smith. 'He said, "Look, if you leave me entirely alone, I'm going to feel abandoned. But I don't want you coming to my desk every day. It makes me nervous. For the next month let me do the daily graph myself and you come and see me on Fridays to check it out. If I need some help during the week, I'll come to see you."'

'So you worked out a new agreement with him', said the veteran. 'Did you keep doing that until he performed like a winner in that part of his job?'

'Absolutely', said Smith. 'I want to supervise my people closely only if they need it. As soon as they can perform on their own, I am ready to let go. In coaching you want to schedule fewer and fewer feedback meetings as people move gradually from their present level of performance to the desired level of performance. We have an expression that we use here, that I think would be important for you to learn.' She wrote on her pad:

*

Achieving
Good Performance
For
Most People
Is
A Journey –
Not
A Destination

*

'That's well put', said the veteran. 'Many managers just shout out destinations (goals) and then sit back and wait for people to reach them. What's helpful about the PRICE system is that it suggests that coaching is a process of managing the journey. I'm ready to move on to *Evaluate* (E), the last step in the PRICE system. Are you?'

'Why not?' said Smith. 'After all, evaluation and coaching go hand in hand. In fact, every time you give someone feedback you are evaluating. You want to continually determine how well performance is going in pinpointed areas. Are you getting the results you want? If not, why?'

'If evaluation and coaching go hand in hand', said the veteran manager, 'why do you have *evaluate* as a separate step in the PRICE system?'

'Because most organisations have actual formal performance review sessions', said the veteran. 'These sessions are held quarterly, semi-annually, or only once a year. In the PRICE system we recommend that you graph and track performance in pinpointed One Minute Goal areas for no longer than six weeks without having a formal evaluation session – unless the person is a proven winner.'

'What do you discuss in these sessions?' wondered the veteran.

'Nothing new', said Smith. 'Remember, praisings and reprimands must be delivered as close to the performance as possible. No saving up. All we do is review what we have been talking about throughout the coaching process. The main question at these evaluation sessions is to decide whether you want to keep the performance area as a PRICE project or assume it is now fixed or accomplished and the people involved can give themselves their own feedback. If the performance is still not up to the desired level, then you start the process again.'

'While evaluation in the PRICE system is a continuous process', said the veteran, 'I don't get the feeling it is a punitive process. In putting One Minute Management to work, you are not trying to trip people up.'

'David Berlo, one of the most thoughtful teachers and consultants I have ever met', said Smith, 'gave me the best expression of that philosophy. He got interested in the training of whales. One day he asked some of his training friends whether they actually trained the whales by using some of the concepts we have been talking about in the coaching process. They said, "Yes, with one addition".'

'What was that?' wondered the veteran.

'Before they attempted to train the whales to do anything', said Smith, 'the trainers told David, "We feed them and make sure they're not hungry. And then we jump in the water and play with the whales until we have convinced them . . ."'

'Convinced them of what?' wondered the veteran manager.

'Let me write that down for you', said Smith, 'because it underlies everything that One Minute Management stands for'. She reached over and borrowed the veteran manager's notepad and began to write.

*

We
Mean
Them
No
Harm

*

'That's a powerful statement', said the veteran manager as he read what Alice Smith had written. 'That's all about trust, isn't it?'

'It certainly is', said Smith. 'David is writing a book entitled *I Mean You No Harm* because he feels that most of the performance review and evaluation systems that companies set up in our country suggest the very opposite.'

'Now that you mention it', said the veteran, 'that is so true. Most evaluation systems suggest that there always have to be winners and losers.'

'That's just not part of the philosophy of the One Minute Manager', said Smith.

'So when you talk about evaluation in the PRICE system', said the veteran, 'you are always trying to find out whether you are getting the desired results. If you are, your staff get recognised and praised. And if you're not, they get re-directed or reprimanded depending on whether the problem is one of ability or motivation. Are there any other reasons why you wouldn't be getting the desired results?'

'Performance can break down at every step of the PRICE system', responded Smith. 'You might have pinpointed an irrelevant area. Or you might be recording data ineffectively. In involving your staff you might have agreed upon too low or too high a goal, your feedback might be erratic or your consequences not sufficiently motivating.'

'So you are taking some significant responsibility for ensuring that your staff perform well', said the veteran manager.

'Most definitely', said Smith. 'My job as a manager is not just to sit back, cross my arms, look stern and evaluate. It's to roll up my sleeves and be responsive to people and what they need to perform well.'

'So you have to keep your eyes and ears open', interjected the veteran. 'I would imagine you often go back to Pinpoint, and start the process again. So PRICE is a continuous process.'

'Exactly', said Smith. 'That's why we like to show PRICE almost like a dial on the telephone', she said, pointing to a plaque on the wall. It read:

A Summary of
the
PRICE SYSTEM

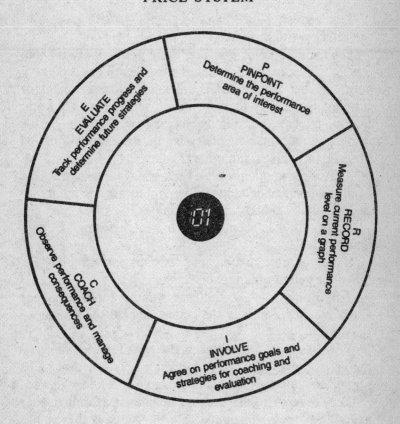

'That's great. Now I can dial 'P' for performance', said the veteran with a smile.

'Let me emphasise one last thing about PRICE', said Smith. 'You can use it to achieve excellence in all parts of your life. Set up a PRICE system for losing weight or running. Set one up for your kids' chores or school work. If you involve your family you can make New Year's resolutions become a reality rather than another unfulfilled promise to yourself and others.'

'It gives me another way to take what I know about One Minute Management and really put it to work in an organised fashion', said the veteran manager.

'It certainly has been the key to our performance', said Smith.

'Have you ever had anyone resist paying the PRICE?' asked the veteran manager.

'Why don't you ask the One Minute Manager about Chris?' smiled Smith as she got up and led the veteran to the door.

'Yes, I suppose I have taken enough of your time', said the veteran manager. 'I've found this very practical and I appreciate your willingness to share your secrets with me.'

'They're secrets only because people act as though they never knew them', responded Smith. 'Actually they're just common sense put to use.'

As the veteran walked back to the One Minute Manager's office, he was amazed at how true that phrase was – common sense put to use.

When he got to the One Minute Manager's office, the veteran was greeted with a warm smile. 'The PRICE is right, isn't it?' the One Minute Manager laughed.

'It certainly is', said the veteran manager. 'It really makes sense, but I have one question. Who is Chris?'

The One Minute Manager began to laugh. 'I thought it was only a matter of time before someone told you about Chris. Why don't you sit down', said the One Minute Manager, 'so I can tell you about Chris'.

'When I first came here I heard about Chris from Steve Mulvany, a productivity-improvement consultant who had worked with our company. Steve said, "Watch out for Chris when you start training the foremen about One Minute Management. He's a real tough guy." I got the impression that converting Chris to One Minute Management would be like persuading a charging rhino to rethink his strategy.

'The stories about Chris were widespread. He was almost a legend in his own time. For instance, I was told that one time he was so enraged by one of his staff in the morning that he literally (I checked it out later with Chris and it was true) picked him up and hung him by his overalls on a nail and left him there until lunch.'

'Now, how could anybody do that?' asked the veteran manager.

'Chris is about five feet nine by five feet nine and strong', said the One Minute Manager. 'When he sits at the end of our thirty-inch-wide conference table he is about as wide as the table. He has arms as big as my thighs. His head sits on his shoulders as if he had no neck.'

'He doesn't sound like a very attractive human being', said the veteran.

'No, he's not – or at least he wasn't', said the One Minute Manager. 'His eyes were bloodshot, he had a grumpy voice, and he walked like a bear on the prowl.

'I first met Chris', continued the One Minute Manager, 'at a training session. When I came here and began to implement One Minute Management, I initially did most of the training myself. I arrived early to the session where I met Chris. While I was setting up training materials in the front of the conference room, I suddenly got the feeling somebody was watching me. I turned round and there was Chris sitting alone at the other end of the conference room.'

'How did you know it was him?' asked the veteran manager.

'I just knew', said the One Minute Manager. 'Especially when I got no response to a smile. I could just feel his eyes looking through me.'

'What did you say?' interrupted the veteran. 'I feel as if I'm in the middle of another soap opera.'

'Nothing then', said the One Minute Manager, 'but I knew he was watching my every move. At least I sensed he was. When I started my session he sat quietly until I said, "One of the keys to motivating your people is to catch them doing something right. When that occurs", I asked, "what should you do as a manager?" Everyone said reward or praise them, except Chris.'

'How did you know he didn't agree?' said the veteran manager.

'Chris raised his hand', said the One Minute Manager, 'and I thought to myself, "Well, the session is over. Pack your bags." He said, "I want to say something" and I said, "Go ahead".

'Chris said, "I just want you to know that I use punishment and it works".

'I looked at him and thought to myself, "What are you going to say to someone like Chris?" He could have said that the sky was green and I would have agreed straight away that the sky was green.

'When I regained my composure, I said, "That's interesting, Chris. Would you be willing to tell the others in the group what the advantages of punishment are?"

'He said, "Of course! There are three: it's easy; it's fast; and it makes me feel good."

'Looking at his size, I said to myself, "I'll bet it works for you". Then I said, "If those are the advantages, Chris, are there any drawbacks to using too much punishment?"

'Chris smiled and said, "I can't think of one".

'I said, "I can think of three areas too much punishment can affect – efficiency rates, absenteeism, and staff turnover".

'Chris stared at me because he knew what I was thinking. He had the lowest efficiency rates in the plant. Now he knew that but I had heard his excuses: "I have the toughest department", and "I'm on a swing shift and everyone knows that swing shifts traditionally have the lowest productivity".

'Absenteeism – Chris consistently had 20 per cent of his staff absent so he had eight out of ten at work most days. The personnel people joked that without Chris's department they would have to lay off one staff member. They were busy every day processing transfer requests, resignations, or hiring for his department.

'Staff turnover – his was the highest in the plant. But I had heard him say, "I manage the worst department there is and everyone likes to get out of it as soon as possible".

'When it was obvious I was baiting him, Chris said, "OK, boss. How do you expect me to work differently with the bunch of layabouts I've got working for me? They live to pay for their booze. And besides, I don't like them and they don't like me."

'I said, "Chris, I know you probably think these sessions are a waste of time. But will you give me a chance?"

'"OK!" said Chris. "But I'm not counting on anything."

'After I had talked about the need to start any perform-ance-improvement programme with pinpointing the prob-lem and then recording present performance, I discussed the importance of the daily printout from the computer for checking progress and giving people feedback. You see, in our operation the foremen get good information on performance.'

'As you were speaking, what was Chris doing?' asked the veteran manager.

'He just sat there with his arms crossed', said the One Minute Manager. 'There was no expression on his face.'

'After the meeting, much to my surprise, Chris came up to me and said, "Look, I think this stuff is probably useless, but I'd like to increase my efficiency rate. Any ideas?"

'"Every day you get a printout from the computer on the efficiency of each of your machines for the day before", I replied. "Since you have a one man per machine operation, this information tells you how each of your men is doing. All I want you to do is make a graph for everyone and, at the beginning of every morning, fill in the efficiency ratings on the graphs and then walk around and show each man what his efficiency was from the day before. That's all I want you to do."

'"OK", said Chris. "I'll give it a try even though I don't think it will work."

'The next morning, I went down to see what happened', continued the One Minute Manager. 'Chris got the printout from the computer and transferred the information to graphs for each of his staff and then walked over to his first man and said, "Listen, don't give me any crap about the number on here. Just look at it." And then he showed the man his efficiency rating.

'I thought to myself, "This is going to be a disaster", so I told Chris to simply show them the number and not to say anything else. I told him to say merely "You got 86 per cent efficiency yesterday". "You got 94." "You got 100."

'When he said to the next man, "You got 83 per cent efficiency yesterday", the man said, "Chris, get out of here and get away from me. We're going to call the union. Leave us alone. You've left us alone for years unless we did something wrong, so just get out of here."

'Chris said to me, "I told you they don't like me".

'I said, "Chris, keep trying".

'Chris kept showing his men their efficiency rates even though they were giving him a hard time and not even looking at their graphs. Then after about four days I could see them starting to look when he came along showing them their scores. They were starting to look at the graphs because they were beginning to get feedback and were able to compare how they did yesterday to the day before, and the day before that.'

'And the comparisons were against themselves, not the other men', interrupted the veteran manager.

'Yes', said the One Minute Manager. 'We find it more constructive to have people competing against themselves and a performance standard rather than competing with each other.'

'What happened next?' asked the veteran manager, anxious to get back to hearing about Chris.

'Chris told his staff, "Listen, I'm getting sick and tired of giving this feedback to you all. From now on, if anybody has 85 per cent or higher efficiency, I'll come and show you your rating. But if you didn't get 85 per cent, you don't deserve to talk to me." '

'Let's see if I can fit this story into the PRICE system', suggested the veteran. 'When Chris said he wanted to improve efficiency he was pinpointing the problem. That's *P*. When he made the graphs from the computer printout he was up to *R* for record. And when he began showing his men their efficiency ratings in the beginning he was involving them, even if he was a little autocratic. That's *I*. Now by deciding to talk only with people with 85 per cent or higher efficiency, it sounds as if Chris was beginning to manage consequences and to coach. That's *C*. That decision was made at his own kind of evaluation session: *E*.'

'Exactly!' said the One Minute Manager. 'You really learned the PRICE system quickly, didn't you?'

'I just love the simplicity of it all', said the veteran manager.

'It was funny to see Chris', continued the One Minute Manager, 'walk up to a man and then, reading that his efficiency rate was below 85, walk straight past him without showing him his graph or saying a word. The expression on that person's face was priceless. He acted as if Chris had stabbed him in the back.'

'I bet pretty soon everyone was getting over 85 per cent efficiency', said the veteran manager.

'You're quite right', said the One Minute Manager. 'After a week or so Chris called them all together again. He said, "You've got to achieve 95 per cent efficiency or I don't come to your machine". It was amazing how their efficiency scores climbed.'

'That's amazing, considering that all Chris was doing was giving them the information', said the veteran.

'Right', said the One Minute Manager. 'He didn't say they did well; he didn't say they did badly. Just the fact that Chris would show up at their machines was important to them.

'He did this', continued the One Minute Manager, 'for some time. Then, after about a month, he gave each of them their own graph and stopped coming to their machines but he would leave the printout from the computer on his desk. I swear to you, nine out of ten of the men would run over there during their break time to see what they got and go back and fill in their graphs.'

'Then he started to circle in red the names of those men who got 95 per cent. Can you believe it? A bunch of hard-nosed types like this talking about whether they got a red circle that day. They thought it was really something special if they got a red circle.'

'What was happening to the performance in Chris's department all this time?' asked the veteran manager.

'It was going up like a spaceship on the graph', said the One Minute Manager. 'At the same time his absenteeism and tardiness were going down too. The other foremen didn't believe it. They thought Chris was cheating about the data. I knew he wasn't because I was watching the data all the time.'

'What did he do next?' said the veteran manager.

'One day', said the One Minute Manager, 'he brought all his staff together and said, "You men have really been increasing your efficiency. I'll tell you what I'll do. My wife makes the best chocolate cake you've ever tasted so if everyone in this department gets 100 per cent or higher today, I'll bring in some of her chocolate cake tomorrow for everyone."

'I wasn't at the meeting but I heard about it through the grapevine. I went to see him. I said, "Chris, chocolate cake as a motivator? It's not going to work."

'He said, "That's what you think. Let me do it."

'I said, "Chris, you can do anything you want" – as if I could stop him'.

'Chris didn't even walk around and watch them', continued the One Minute Manager. 'They monitored themselves. For example, the biggest man in the department started walking around and saying things like "Jim, you'd better get 100 per cent". "Joe, you'd better get 100 per cent. . . ." If someone left his machine to get something or do something, one of the men would yell, "Hey, where are you going? You get back to work."'

'Did everyone get 100 per cent efficiency?' asked the veteran manager.

'Too right', said the One Minute Manager. 'No exceptions. So at lunchtime the next day Chris brought in these plates of chocolate cake. You never saw anything go so fast in your life. They loved it.

'I thought that was something, so I decided to try out the idea on the other departments.

'I called in my key staff and told them I would be willing to buy lunch the next day for every department that got 100 per cent or higher in efficiency on any given day'.

'What did your staff think?' asked the veteran manager.

'Everyone thought it was a great idea', said the One Minute Manager. 'We had these little vouchers printed up that the employees could use on the "roach coach".'

'The roach coach?' wondered the veteran manager.

'That's an affectionate name for the food trolley that goes around, selling all kinds of goodies', said the One Minute Manager. 'Our staff often wait to eat lunch until it arrives.'

'While I thought my plan was a good idea, it went down like a lead balloon. In fact, people got hostile. They were saying things like: "This is ridiculous!" "Don't expect us to work ourselves into the ground for a free lunch voucher. We're insulted."'

'What happened?' asked the veteran manager.

'I was confused', said the One Minute Manager, 'so I asked Chris to come and see me'.

'So Chris is now a consultant to top management', laughed the veteran.

'It took courage to admit I needed advice from Chris', confessed the One Minute Manager.

'What did Chris think of the programme?' wondered the veteran manager.

'He had elected not to do the voucher programme', said the One Minute Manager. 'In fact, he was one of the leaders of the revolt. That's why I wanted to talk to him – to find out why he wouldn't participate in the voucher programme.

'When Chris arrived at my office, I asked him, "Why aren't you involved in the voucher programme?"

'Chris leaned over to me and put his finger right in my face and said, "You tried to bribe the employees. You offered them a free voucher on the roach coach to increase productivity. Let me tell you how I and the other men felt about that. We were mad. We felt used and insulted."

'Then he took his finger away from my face, paused, and stared in my eyes for what seemed like an endless moment. "Let me tell you one other thing", Chris said as he broke the silence. "You're good. You've done a tremendous job putting the One Minute Manager to work here. We think you're better than that kind of bribery stuff."

'Then Chris smiled and said, "How's that for a One Minute Reprimand?"

'I have to admit that being on the end of a reprimand from Chris wasn't the most comfortable experience I've ever had', said the One Minute Manager.

'After I got my composure back, I said, "I realise I made a mistake, but how was what I did different from what you did with the chocolate cake?"

' "My wife made that chocolate cake", said Chris. "I put myself out and so did she. You offered to give us a free lunch voucher to use on the roach coach. That's an insult and a bribe."

' "So my lunch voucher", I said, "was insulting because it wasn't personal and it didn't involve any emotional commitment from me?"

' "Right", said Chris. "You have done a fantastic job here, introducing your concepts of One Minute Management and teaching us the ABC's. Most of us are willing to pay the PRICE to get good performance. The people who work for you are winners and you shouldn't take the ball away from them. Don't try to sprinkle reinforcement from on high."

' "I understand what you are saying, Chris", I replied, "and I really want to thank you for your honesty".

' "That's OK", said Chris. "I've learned a lot here and there's no reason why I can't help you learn, too."

'We both smiled and shook hands.'

'Chris is quite a guy, isn't he?' said the veteran manager.

'He certainly is', said the One Minute Manager. 'It's people like him who have really made our efforts worthwhile here.'

'And he's taught me to put the things I've learned here into a human perspective', added the veteran. 'Speaking of the things I've learned, I'd like to sum it all up for you. I want to be certain I've got it all straight.'

'Go ahead', said the One Minute Manager.

'First, I cleared up some questions I had about the three secrets of One Minute Management: One Minute Goal Setting, One Minute Praisings and One Minute Reprimands', remembered the veteran manager. 'Second, I've learned that the ABC's of Management (the Activators, the resulting Behaviour and the appropriate Consequences) help sequence those secrets in a way that makes them usable. And third, the PRICE System gives me a good basic knowledge of how to put the One Minute Manager to work in a systematic way that can be shared with everyone. It turns the secrets into skills and moves the application of One Minute Management beyond individuals to work groups and the organisation as a whole.'

The One Minute Manager smiled as he listened to the veteran. He loved to see the excitement that learning new things sparked in people.

'Sounds as if you have everything pretty straight', commented the One Minute Manager.

'I think I've got it', said the veteran. 'I can't thank you enough for sharing with me what you know and have learned about management.'

'It's my pleasure', said the One Minute Manager. 'All that knowledge is to be shared. Let me leave you with one last thought. The best way to learn to be a One Minute Manager and to use what you have learned is to start to do it. The important thing is not that you do it right, but that you start to do it.'

'I'm really committed to that', said the veteran.

'It's not your commitment that I'm worried about', said the One Minute Manager. 'It's your commitm. nt to your commitment. For example, people say diets don't work. Diets work just fine – it's people who don't work. They break their commitment to their commitment to lose weight. I don't want you to do that with putting the One Minute Manager to work.'

'What you're saying makes sense of what a friend of mine told me', said the veteran. 'He told me I should give up trying. I should either do it or not do it.'

'That's just what I was getting at', said the One Minute Manager. 'To illustrate it, would you try to pick up that pen on the desk?'

The veteran went over to the desk and picked up the pen.

'I told you to try to pick up the pen. I didn't tell you to pick it up', said the One Minute Manager.

The veteran smiled.

'You've got it', said the One Minute Manager. 'You're either going to do it or not going to do it. Saying, "I'll try", just sets up all your past patterns which will result in your not doing it.'

'Thanks for that final advice', said the veteran. 'I certainly don't want to be the man hanging onto the branch on the side of the mountain, yelling, "Is there anybody else up there?"'

With that said, the veteran got up and put his hand out to the One Minute Manager. 'I'm going to do it', he said with sincerity.

WHEN the veteran manager left the One Minute Manager's office, he was excited about implementing what he had learned. He was committed to his commitment to putting the One Minute Manager to work.

The next day he began to do just that. He did not wait until he could do everything he had learned exactly right. He knew if he waited he would never get started, so he shared what he had learned with all his staff, and they in turn shared it with their staff. They all supported one another's efforts to put the secrets of One Minute Management to work.

As he worked with his staff, the veteran manager learned that four systems needed to be set up in the organisation to make One Minute Management pay off. Employees needed to know: what they were being asked to do (accountability system); what good behaviour looked like (performance data system); how well they were doing (feedback system); and what recognition they would get for good performance (recognition system).

Because of his efforts and willingness to share what he had learned, everyone in the veteran manager's organisation set up PRICE projects for each of their One Minute Goals. The goals themselves identified the *pinpointed* areas of interest. Present performance on each of these goals was *recorded*. Then each employee was *involved* in goal setting, as well as establishing coaching and counselling strategies. Then *coaching* began. Managers were responsive to their staff's needs for supervision. Everybody wanted each other to win. When it came to *evaluation* progress was reviewed and new goals set.

Pretty soon the inevitable happened:

The Veteran Manager was Successful
In Putting The One Minute Manager
To Work And It Made A Difference.

People not only felt better, they performed better. And more importantly, putting the One Minute Manager to work made a difference where it really counted – on the bottom line. Production increased, quality improved, sales skyrocketed, and retention and attendance of employees surpassed all the companies in the area.

Everywhere the veteran manager went he shared what he had learned with others. One Minute Management soon became known as Theory W. The One Minute Manager said, 'You can have your Theory X, Theory Y, and Theory Z. We call One Minute Management "Theory W" because it works.'

Wherever the veteran manager went, he always told people who had learned how to put the One Minute Manager to work . . .

*

*Keep Your
Commitment
To
Your Commitment
And
Share
It
With
Others*

*

About the Authors

Dr. Kenneth H. Blanchard, co-developer of the One Minute Manager and Situational Leadership, is an internationally known author, educator and consultant/trainer, and professor of Leadership and Organisational Behaviour at the University of Massachusetts, Amherst. He has written extensively in the field of leadership, motivation and managing change including the widely used and acclaimed Prentice-Hall text, *Management of Organisational Behaviour: Utilising Human Resources*, co-authored with Paul Hersey and now in its fourth edition, and the national best-seller, *The One Minute Manager* (William Collins) co-authored with Spencer Johnson, M.D

Dr. Blanchard received his B.A. in government and philosophy from Cornell University, an M.A. in sociology and counselling from Colgate University, and a Ph.D. in administration and management from Cornell University.

As chairman of the board of Blanchard Training and Development, Inc., a human resource development company, Dr. Blanchard has trained 50,000 managers and has advised a wide range of corporations and agencies. His approaches to management have been incorporated into many Fortune 500 companies as well as numerous fast-growing entrepreneurial companies.

Dr. Robert L. Lorber, an internationally known and recognised expert in performance improvement, is president of RL Lorber and Associates, Inc., a company specialising in the strategic design and implementation of productivity improvement systems, based in Orange, California.

Dr. Lorber received his B.A. and M.A. degrees from the University of California at Davis and in 1974 was awarded a Ph.D. in Applied Behavioural Science and Organisational Psychology. His numerous publications include *Effective Feedback: The Key to Engineering Performance, Managing Data vs Gut Feeling, How to Implement Change: Supervise and Lead,* and *Productivity – in Five Intensive Lessons.*

Dr. Lorber has spoken at many Young Presidents' Organisation universities and area conferences. He is on the board of the Business School at the University of Santa Clara, the Board of Editors of the *Journal of Organisational Behaviour Management,* The Presidents Association of the American Management Association, the American Productivity Management Association, the American Psychological Association, and the World Affairs Council.

Dr. Lorber and his organisation have implemented productivity systems for small, medium and numerous Fortune 500 companies throughout the United States, as well as the Middle East, South America, Mexico, Africa, Europe, and Canada.

Concept Praisings

We would like to acknowledge and give a public praising to the following people whose conceptual contributions were most valuable to us in the course of preparing this book:

David Berlo for his thoughtful analysis of why organisations are not good places for people to be.

Tom Connellan, Aubrey Daniels, and *Larry Miller* for teaching us many things about productivity improvement.

Werner Erhard for what his teachings taught us about making life work and keeping your commitments.

Paul Hersey for being one of the most creative behavioural scientists we know and for his pioneer work on Situational Leadership.

Fred Luthans and *Robert Kreitner* for the first conceptualisation of the ABC's.

Abraham Maslow for the recognition that people's behaviour is driven by different needs at different times.

David McClelland for his pioneer work on achievement motivation and the importance of setting moderately difficult but achievable goals.

Scott Meyers for his outstanding work on understanding and motivating people.

George Odiorne for being 'Mister Management by Objective' (MBO) and for identifying the problems of the 'activity trap'.

B. F. Skinner for his classic work on reinforcement theory.

Rick Tate for his skill in teaching management and coining the phrase 'Feedback Is the Breakfast of Champions'.